JOEY

The Story of Joe Biden

JILL BIDEN

WITH KATHLEEN KRULL

ILLUSTRATED BY AMY JUNE BATES

A PAULA WISEMAN BOOK
SIMON & SCHUSTER BOOKS FOR YOUNG READERS
NEW YORK   LONDON   TORONTO   SYDNEY   NEW DELHI

ILLUSTRATOR ACKNOWLEDGMENTS

I would like to thank Joe Biden for his long service to the public and
Jill Biden for her inspiring telling of his story. Paula Wiseman brought
her great experience to this project and I am grateful for her insights.
Finally, I would like to express my deep appreciation for Laurent Linn.

ILLUSTRATOR'S NOTE

I have been fortunate that the Biden family has shared so many great
images of young Joe with the public. They helped me imagine his
childhood, fun spirit, care for others, and his development into a leader.

Photo on bibliography page by James Jaquet, used with permission.
All other photos from the Biden family collection. All rights reserved.

SIMON & SCHUSTER BOOKS FOR YOUNG READERS
An imprint of Simon & Schuster Children's Publishing Division
1230 Avenue of the Americas, New York, New York 10020
Text copyright © 2020 by Jill Biden
Illustrations copyright © 2020 by Amy June Bates
All rights reserved, including the right of reproduction in whole or in part in any form.
SIMON & SCHUSTER BOOKS FOR YOUNG READERS is a trademark of Simon & Schuster, Inc.
For information about special discounts for bulk purchases,
please contact Simon & Schuster Special Sales at 1-866-506-1949 or business@simonandschuster.com.
The Simon & Schuster Speakers Bureau can bring authors to your live event. For more information or to book an event,
contact the Simon & Schuster Speakers Bureau at 1-866-248-3049 or visit our website at www.simonspeakers.com.
Book design by Laurent Linn
The text for this book was set in Chaparral Pro.
The illustrations for this book were rendered in watercolor, gouache, and pencil.
Manufactured in the United States of America
0620 LAK
2 4 6 8 10 9 7 5 3
CIP data for this book is available from the Library of Congress.
ISBN 978-1-5344-8053-7
ISBN 978-1-5344-8054-4 (eBook)

"Give me the ball!"

    At eight years old, Joey Biden was *always* ready
for the ball. It didn't matter if he was the smallest
boy on the team—baseball, football, basketball,
whatever. No one was more competitive.

    One day he ran into a group of older boys playing
football in an alley. "You can't catch me," he taunted.

    He was right, they couldn't. So they welcomed
him into their game.

Everything was a contest to Joey and his three buddies, Charlie, Larry, and Tommy. It could be as ordinary as walking down the streets of Scranton, Pennsylvania. Which boy could walk the fastest?

But Joey was also a peacemaker who noticed what he and other kids had in common. He often found himself the leader in a club or when playing fort.

Even at age eight, he looked out for others. When his friend's father left for a weeklong fishing trip, Joey went to visit his friend's mom. He promised to take care of her while her husband was away. After getting his own mother's permission, he stayed the whole week, making sure doors and windows were locked at night.

He and his buddies romped
through the neighborhood with
Joey's faithful dogs—a beagle,
Snoopy, and a German shepherd,
King. They pooled their pennies
and dropped in at the candy store where the owner kept a pet monkey.

They headed to the theater for the double feature—a western, maybe,
or a Tarzan movie. On the way home they reenacted thrilling scenes,
hopping from rooftop to rooftop of the garages.

Or they pretended the ground was a seething swamp—"Touch it and
you die—eaten by alligators!" they screamed.

Joey wouldn't dream of missing a water-balloon fight or a snowball battle.

Always eager to prove he had guts, he never refused a dare, even when it was dangerous. He climbed atop a mountain of still-burning coal, for example. He raced along the pipes high above a river. Once he grabbed a heavy rope and swung over a construction site, imitating Tarzan—without a net.

All the neighborhood kids competed to see who could climb the flagpole in the football field. The feat was impossible—the slippery pole swayed in the wind.

Only one kid made it to the top, and that was Joey Biden.

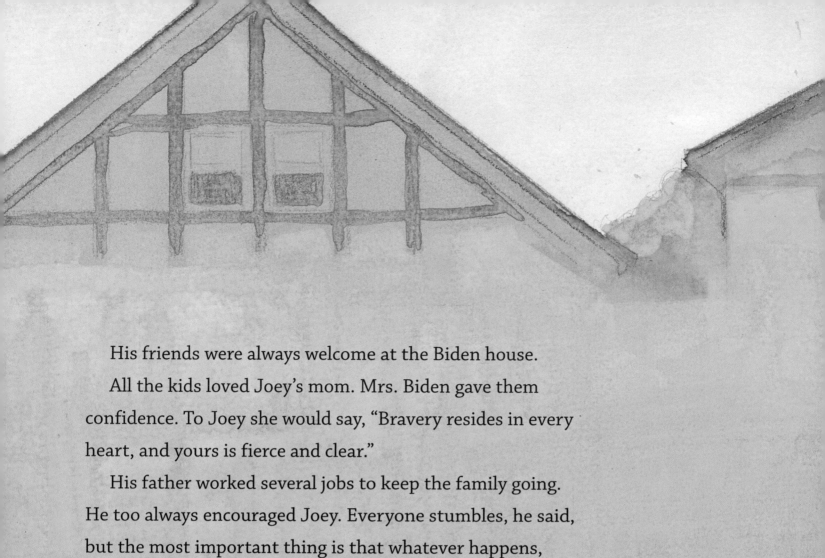

His friends were always welcome at the Biden house.

All the kids loved Joey's mom. Mrs. Biden gave them confidence. To Joey she would say, "Bravery resides in every heart, and yours is fierce and clear."

His father worked several jobs to keep the family going. He too always encouraged Joey. Everyone stumbles, he said, but the most important thing is that whatever happens, "Get up! Get up!"

Family fortunes were up and down. To
find work, Mr. Biden moved the family
from Scranton and eventually to Delaware.
Moving could be difficult, but Joey was lucky
to have his brothers, Jim and Frank, and his
sister, Valerie, who was also his best friend.

Joey and Val were so close that they could finish each other's sentences. As soon as she was old enough, he'd say to Val, "Okay, hop on!" He'd scoop her up on his bike handlebars and take her to any playground she wanted. He taught her all his best sports moves, urging her to keep up with him and his buddies.

As the oldest, Joey took the lead with his siblings. He, Val, and their two younger brothers made a deal with their parents. The kids could settle their own arguments among themselves, closing the door until they resolved them.

The whole family had a rule—if you said, "I give you my word as a Biden," it meant you were telling the absolute truth.

Often after dinner, Joey biked down to the drugstore to get everyone a half gallon of vanilla ice cream to eat while watching *Lassie* and their other favorite shows on TV.

Home was a place for family and learning. His uncle sat Joey down with the newspaper editorial pages and discussed the latest news.

Sunday was always family church day. After Mass the grown-ups sat around the kitchen table to talk politics and sports, and Joey did too.

But school was where the bullies were.

Joey's mind was always sharp and fast, but talking was sometimes really difficult. He stuttered. The words just would not come out smoothly. "Joey, it's because you're so bright," his mother would tell him. "You can't get the thoughts out quickly enough."

Kids made fun of him with cruel nicknames. They assumed he wasn't smart. Joey felt incredibly frustrated, but he remembered his father's words—"Get up. Get up."

Instead of showing how hurt he felt, he fought with boys who teased him.

And he also defended others from bullies, keeping an eye out for kids who were being made fun of.

He took heart from his mother's words: "Remember, Joey, you're a Biden. Nobody is better than you. You're not better than anyone else, but *nobody* is any better than you."

Joey started thinking of ways to help himself talk more smoothly.

Reading out loud in class was his biggest fear. When he knew his turn was coming, he took care to count the desks in advance and figure out which passage he'd be called upon to recite. Then he would memorize it, practicing when to pause, pretending that he was reading out loud.

He noticed that planning ahead helped. As a paperboy delivering the newspapers, he knew which neighbors along his route were fans of the Yankees. Before he went to collect payment, he would check the sports pages so he could say something about the latest game.

He even tried the famous marble trick he'd read about from ancient Greek philosophers. One day he took ten pebbles from a neighbor's garden, put them in his mouth, and practiced speaking, hoping to strengthen his muscles. He had to stop when he realized he was more likely to swallow the pebbles than anything.

Joey went to Catholic schools where nuns were the teachers. They taught math and history, of course, but also values like playing fair, helping others, and being honest. Nuns even played baseball with him. They did everything to encourage him. They stood up for him when he was bullied, and they offered ideas to help with his speech.

One nun suggested putting a singsong rhythm to his words. So, in his bedroom, Joey began memorizing long passages of Irish poems. While holding a flashlight under his chin in front of the mirror, he recited poetry out loud, studying the movements of his face, trying to stop his muscles from tensing up. Hours of practice seemed to help.

After his father got a better job and the family moved to Claymont, Delaware, Joey looked ahead—or actually, across the street. His deepest wish was to attend the Catholic high school overlooking the Delaware River. This was a stately marble building he could see from afar, the sunlight dancing off its two hundred windows.

But his family couldn't afford the tuition. So he turned his dream into reality by applying for a work-study program. He spent summers painting the school's iron fences and pulling weeds in the formal gardens. And he washed those windows— all two hundred of them—with vinegar and water, drying them with newspapers.

While in high school, he grew a whole foot taller: no longer Joey, but Joe.
A football and basketball star, he didn't have to say "Give me the ball!"
anymore. He even earned a new nickname—"Hands"—for his wizardly
ability to catch the ball. In his senior year he led his football team to an
undefeated season, even dramatically scoring the last touchdown himself.

He was a leader off the field as well—elected class president
during his junior and senior years.

The football team always went to the local diner for hamburgers after games. When the owner refused to let his African American teammate order with the rest of the athletes, Joe led the whole team to leave in protest.

At his high school graduation, he gave the welcome to parents and friends without a hitch. "If you put your mind to something, there's nothing you can't do," he said, having overcome his stuttering.

Not only did he lose his fear of public speaking—he also discovered that he liked it. He wanted to communicate, and he looked for opportunities to do more.

"Give me the ball!"

He was inspired by the leaders of the day who were changing the country. At his presidential inauguration John F. Kennedy had said, "Ask not what your country can do for you—ask what you can do for your country." Joe's dream of his own future took the shape of a life in public service.

He looked up biographies of those elected to the United States Congress, those who made laws and served the people. He didn't know any other Biden who had gone to college, but it would clearly be his next step.

He went on to the University of Delaware, where he was promptly elected president of his freshman class.

He spent one summer as the only white lifeguard at a pool in an all-black neighborhood. This was the time of segregation and the struggle for civil rights. While playing basketball with other lifeguards, Joe learned firsthand about the struggles of black America.

After graduating from law school, Joe had things to say. Maybe he was just a regular guy, not rich, not privileged, but he dreamed big and saw himself as a leader—"the best Biden I can be."

"Give me the ball!" Only now instead of sports it was politics.

In 1972 he launched an unlikely quest to become a senator from Delaware and serve in Congress. He was only twenty-nine—you couldn't even become a senator until you were thirty.

Valerie managed his campaign, and his whole family helped, while he threw himself into speaking with strength about making people's lives better.

"Give me the ball!"—not a real ball, but a job in politics. And voters did. Against all the odds, Joe became one of the youngest people ever elected to the United States Senate.

As a senator he was one of one hundred people who handled serious responsibilities, like voting on what laws the United States should have. He was powerful and respected, always voted "most liked." He was reelected five times

Every day he commuted by train from Washington back and forth to his family in Delaware.

"The absolute most important thing is your family," he always told those who worked for him.

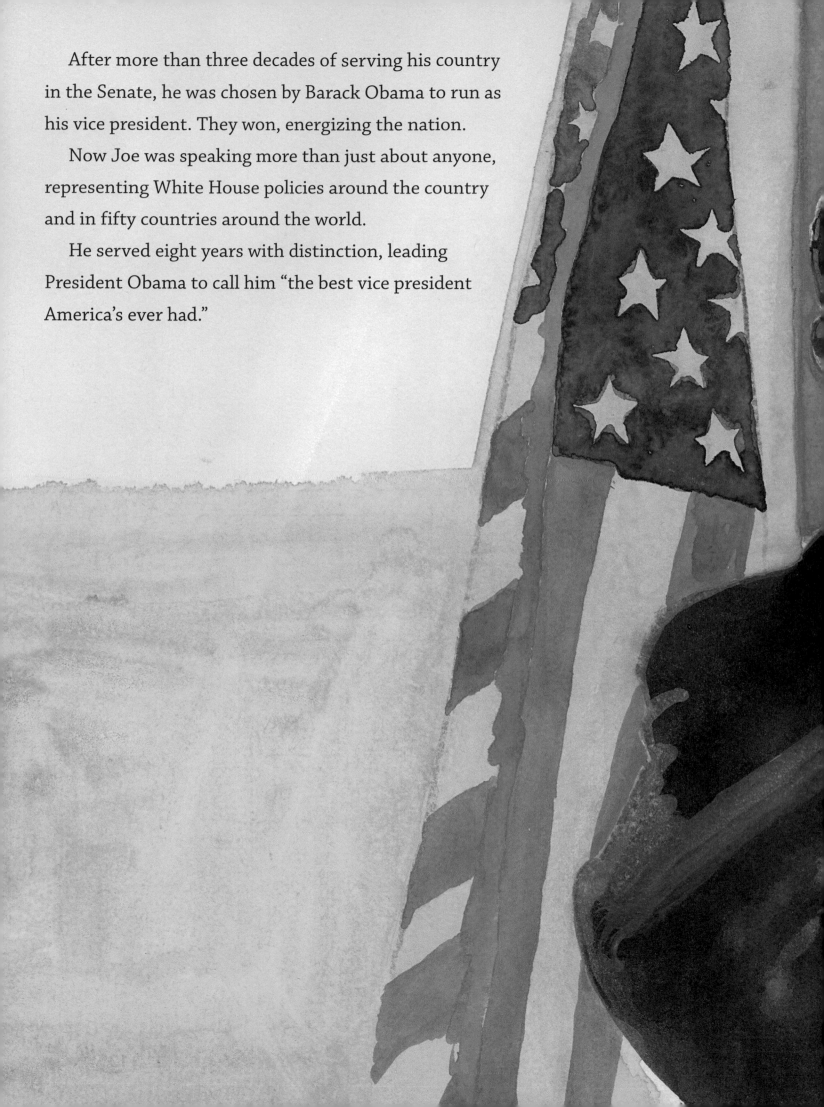

After more than three decades of serving his country in the Senate, he was chosen by Barack Obama to run as his vice president. They won, energizing the nation.

Now Joe was speaking more than just about anyone, representing White House policies around the country and in fifty countries around the world.

He served eight years with distinction, leading President Obama to call him "the best vice president America's ever had."

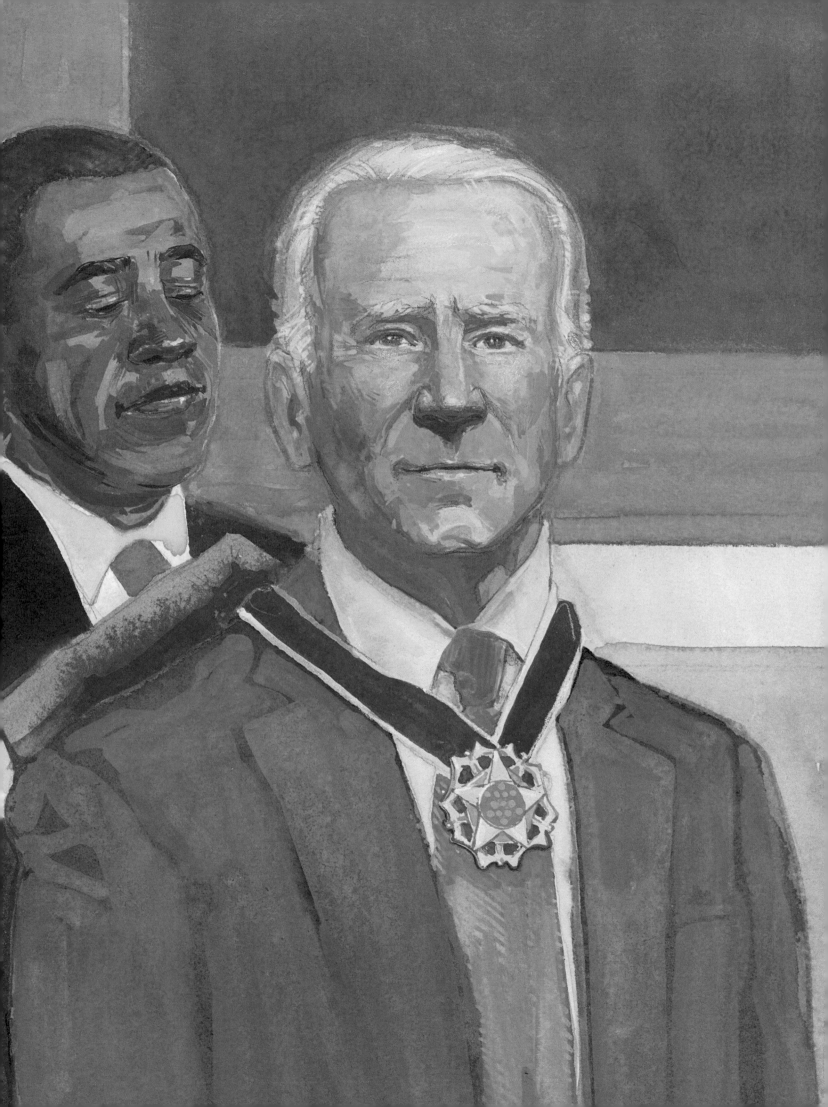

After huddling with his family, he announced in 2019 that he was running for president of the United States. With his decades of experience he called the next election a "battle for the soul of America"—and Joe Biden was ready to fight it.

"Give me the ball!"

A Biden Family Scrapbook

DEC · 54

SOURCES FOR QUOTATIONS

"Give me the ball": Biden, Joseph R. *Promises to Keep* (p. 4).

"You can't catch me": Witcover, Jules. *Joe Biden* (p. 12).

"Touch it and you die": Biden, Joseph R. *Promises to Keep* (p. xii).

"Bravery resides in every heart, and yours is fierce and clear": Barack Obama, Joe Biden Medal of Freedom Presentation Address, https://americanrhetoric.com /speeches/barackobama/barackobamajoebidenmedaloffreedom.htm.

"Get up! Get up!" Biden, Joseph R. *Promises to Keep* (p. xxii).

"Joey, it's because you're so bright": Wilser, Jeff. *The Book of Joe* (p. 4).

"Remember, Joey, you're a Biden": Biden, Joseph R. *Promises to Keep* (p.11).

"Okay, hop on!" Witcover, Jules. *Joe Biden* (p. 15).

"My word as a Biden": Biden, Jill. *Where the Light Enters* (p. 49).

"Hands": Witcover, Jules. *Joe Biden* (p. 23).

"If you put your mind to something": Uschan, Michael V. *Joe Biden* (p. 24).

"Ask not what your country can do for you": John F. Kennedy's Inaugural Address, January 20, 1961, https://www.ushistory.org/documents/ask-not.htm.

"the best Biden I can be": Wilser, Jeff. *The Book of Joe* (p. 124).

"most liked" senator: Biden, Jill. *Where the Light Enters* (p. 155).

"The absolute most important thing": Wilser, Jeff. *The Book of Joe* (p. 156).

"the best vice president America's ever had": Barack Obama, Joe Biden Medal of Freedom Presentation Address, https://americanrhetoric.com/speeches /barackobama/barackobamajoebidenmedaloffreedom.htm.

"battle for the soul of America": https://joebiden.com/joes-vision/.

TIME LINE

November 20, 1942 Joseph Robinette Biden is born in Scranton, Pennsylvania, the oldest of four children.

1953 In search of a job, Joe's father moves the family to an apartment in Claymont, Delaware, and several years later to a house in Wilmington, Delaware.

1961 After being elected class president during his junior and senior years, Joe graduates from Archmere Academy in Claymont.

1965 Receives a bachelor's degree in history and political science from the University of Delaware.

1966 Marries Neilia Hunter and later has three children—Joseph, known as "Beau" (born in 1969); Hunter (1970); and Naomi (1971).

1968 After earning a law degree from Syracuse University in New York, practices law at a law firm and as a public defender.

1969 Enters politics, running for the New Castle County Council and serving until 1972.

1972 Elected to the United States Senate at the age of twenty-nine, becoming the fifth youngest senator in history. Weeks later his wife and baby daughter are killed in a car accident, and his two sons are seriously injured. He was sworn in as senator by his sons' hospital bedside. He never moved to Washington, DC. For his entire Senate career, he commuted from Wilmington to Washington every day, 120 miles round-trip.

1977 Marries Jill Jacobs, a high school English teacher, later a professor of English, and they have a daughter, Ashley (born 1981).

1978 Wins reelection to the Senate, and then five more times, becoming Delaware's longest-serving senator. Among other accomplishments, writes and spearheads the Violence Against Women Act—landmark legislation that criminalizes violence against women.

1988 Pursues presidential nomination without success, also in 2008.

2008 Chosen by Barack Obama to be his vice presidential running mate.

January 20, 2009 Resigns from the Senate shortly before taking the oath of office as vice president. Begins representing Obama's policies to the country and the world, and among other accomplishments, helps secure the passage of the Affordable Care Act, reducing the number of uninsured Americans.

2015 His eldest son, Beau, then attorney general of Delaware, dies from brain cancer at age forty-six.

January 12, 2017 Following the Obama-Biden Administration he launched the Penn Biden Center for Diplomacy and Global Engagement; the University of Delaware Biden Institute: Biden School of Public Policy and Administration; the Biden Foundation; and the Biden Cancer Initiative.

2017 Named the Benjamin Franklin Presidential Practice Professor at the University of Pennsylvania, focusing on foreign policy and national security.

April 2019 Announces his candidacy for president.

March 2020 In the front-runner position for the presidential nomination.

BIBLIOGRAPHY

Barack Obama presents Joe Biden with Presidential Medal of Freedom. Jan. 2017. https://www.youtube.com/watch?v=d3UCW_AV93M.

Biden, Jill. *Where the Light Enters: Building a Family, Discovering Myself.* New York: Flatiron Books, 2019.

Biden, Joseph R. *Promises to Keep: On Life and Politics.* New York: Random House, 2007.

Hendrickson, John. "What Joe Biden Can't Bring Himself to Say." *The Atlantic,* Jan./Feb. 2020.

Hook, Janet. "Joe Biden's Childhood Struggle with a Stutter: How He Overcame It and How It Shaped Him." *Los Angeles Times*, Sept. 16, 2019.

Jedra, Christina. "Wilmington Names Pool after Joe Biden, Former Lifeguard." *Delaware Online*, June 26, 2017. https://www.delawareonline.com/story /news/local/2017/06/26/wilmington-names-pool-after-joe-biden-former -lifeguard/408917001/.

Joe Biden (official website). https://joebiden.com/joes-story.

Kotzwinkle, Bill. Personal (undated) letter to Joe Biden.

Uschan, Michael V. *Joe Biden.* Detroit: Lucent Books, 2010.

Wilser, Jeff. *The Book of Joe: The Life, Wit, and (Sometimes Accidental) Wisdom of Joe Biden.* New York: Three Rivers Press, 2017.

Witcover, Jules. *Joe Biden: A Life of Trial and Redemption*, revised edition. New York: William Morrow, 2019.

If you have to ask, it's too late.

Bravery resides in every heart, and yours is fierce and clear. (Mom)

Joey, when you get knocked down: Get up, get up. (Dad)

A job is about a lot more than a paycheck, it's about your dignity—it's about respect.

Say what you mean and mean what you say.

Out of everything terrible, something good will come if you look hard enough.

America is made of ordinary people capable of extraordinary things.

Progress is never easy, but always possible.

Things do get better on our march toward a more perfect union.

Keep the faith.